Conversations of the Heart

Roohi

BookLeaf
Publishing

India | USA | UK

The Publisher and Editor shall not be liable
whatsoever...

*To emotions that beautifully paint our world—
love, happiness, joy, pain, fear and everything in
between. They shape our life experiences and
make us who we are!*

Acknowledgements

This collection is a journey through emotions, each one drawn from the people who've crossed my path, the friendships that have shaped me and the relationships that have both lifted and broken me. Each poem reflects moments of joy, possibilities, growth and vulnerability – some shared, some quietly felt.

To the friends who've stood by me, offering laughter, comfort and sometimes silence – I carry your words and presence with me, woven into these pages. To the love that has marked my heart, thank you for teaching me what it means to truly feel.

To life itself, with its unexpected turns and lessons – this book is as much a result of your unfolding as it is of my thoughts. You've been both the storm and the calm.

I also want to express my deepest gratitude to
my readers. Your willingness to see yourself in
these words, to share in these emotions,
makes this work alive in ways I never could
have imagined on my own. Without you,
these poems would remain unspoken.

The BookLeaf Publishing house has been
immensely supportive through the process of
ideation to implementation. Thank you for
making this happen

Lastly, to poetry itself: thank you for always
being there when I needed a way to make
sense of the world, for holding space for my
most raw and honest moments and for
turning fragments of thought into something
whole.

This book is as much yours as it is mine.
Thank you for being part of this journey.

Preface

Imagine weaving a beautiful adventure in life, shaping our experience in profound and intense ways. Emotions whisper, sing, scream and yell, asking us to feel, listen and understand this beautiful world around us. The collection of poems in this book gives voices to these emotions... love, happiness, joy, pain, fear and hope – that so often are locked in our hearts.

I have imagined a full spectrum of feelings; every poem is an invitation for you to explore those emotions that are engraved deep within your heart and mind. From smiles that melt hearts to intense silence to waves of passion to embracing vulnerability to celebrating life. You will probably take on your own journey as you find pieces of you smiling, comforting, reciprocating, knowing that we are not alone in this journey

Welcome and embrace this space where
emotions breathe and speak like a free spirit.

Happiness

Like a fleeting breeze, you arrive,
Whispering through the dancing trees,
Your mysterious touch embraces the heart,
A gentle pull from deep within,
Knocking my soul, you leave no trace,
Warmth so quiet with tender grace.

As the sun rays tickle the skin
Playing in the stillness of the dawn,
Drawing hope and light all the while,
Crocheting magic in golden threads
A prayer, a walk, a smile, a dance,
Life's main stage for a play to start.

It lives in smiles that light the eyes,
In stolen glances, joyful sighs,
In playful games, in romantic gaze,
In winding roads and mysterious clouds.
In sunsets painting evening skies,
Watching to see how time flies.

In simple joys that bloom each day,
In little things, it finds its way–
The taste of rain, the scent of petrichor,
The warmth of hands that intertwine.
The connecting hearts in a hug,
Precious moments to plug.

In the warmth of love,
In little acts of kindness,
Touching hearts, happy minds,
A place where joy and sorrow part.
A universe full of fine thoughts,
A piece that can't be bought.

Can be felt, can be seen,
Like a spell that magic brings
In those moments, brief but bright,
It fills the world with endless light.
A touch that's here to stay,
Isn't it life's true way!

Love

Can I be the first one
To whisper good morning in your ears,
While the morning light gently plays in your
eyes,
And paint the dawn in hues,
Adorning your sun-kissed face.

Can I be the first one to hold your hand,
Intertwined in energy.
Connecting hearts, minds and body
In the softest light, with the deepest care.

To walk beside you, through winding streams,
Through mountains.
Through rivers and snow,
Watching the skies,
To be singing in a daze,
Weaving timeless love tale.

To share with you, your desires
To walk beside you like a shadow

With every step, as our hearts beat for each
other
Through joy, hopes and tears

To catch your glance,
When you meet me, midst friends.
To feel the warmth in your smiles,
To reflect through your eyes,
To trace the path where our hearts expand.

To call you mine and only mine,
In a universe of endless galaxies,
For in your eyes, the stars align,
In your smiles, life thrives,
In a cosmic dance, vivid as the universe.

To hold your gaze,
To feel your long sighs,
In moments of intense longing,
To feel your heart,
Listen to the rhythm,
A song only I could know.

To hold you closest,
As twilight fades and stars begin to glow,

Embracing the tight hugs,
To feel those intense kisses,
To let emotions flow like the Ganges,
In the silence, where the words don't play,
Every cell resonates with love's soaring grace.

To cross the realms,
In the stillness where only truth remains,
And in your arms, I am forever claimed,
Waiting long, for you to cross.
For in your soul, I see I found a little place
Meant to be just for me,
Happy, calm yet wild and free!!

Passion

In moments of deep calling, it wakes,
A flicker, a flame, a spark,
It stirs in the heart, deep in the soul,
A longing to reach, to achieve more.

It whispers in dreams and speaks when awake,
Guiding like wind that is ready to bind.
Steady steps, both light and bold,
Unfurling its wings, and
Ready to soar.

It flows like a river, swift and clear,
Rushes with joy and conquers fear.
Through mountains of doubt, through peaks
of pain,
It battles around like an untamed whirlwind.

The fire in the eyes, the unyielding hand,
builds, destroys and rebuilds.
A journey unmarked,
Moments of triumph and trial blend.

For passion is boundless with possibilities
unknown,
Immeasurable force, a tough heart unnamed.
It never grows weary; it never stands still,
It burns bright with relentless will.

So follow its pathway my friend, wherever it
takes,
Through stormy nights and through endless
meads.
For this journey is life's true art,
And its light forever ignites the heart.

Awe

I often wondered as a child
Of a jumbo velvet blanket
Did someone adorn it with
Stars, moons, auroras...
Casting a magical spell – Glitter, bling n
shine!!
And the universe turned into a masterpiece!

Today beneath the endless silver sky,
From distant balconies, we gaze,
Your eyes meet mine in silver light,
The moon feels so close, and our story so new!
Guided by love in the moon's soft light
Wrapping me warm, midst the cold night
skies
Casting its glow upon my face,
Turns this moment into grace,
A tender peace, a quiet ease,
A perfect silence – that's how it feels.

I smile and I wonder
Of loving you to the moon and back.

From here to stars that light the night
I'd fly; I'd chase your heart across the sky,
Parachute back with all my might,
For a moment with you,
Is worth the universe, times two.

Time drifts watching the endless sky,
Distance is an imagination.
Your presence around me,
Flirtatious as the moon.
In your gaze, I clearly see,
A timeless bond in celestial flight,
Embracing it together in our hearts,
Magnificent super moon's here to stay
Two souls, one glow,
Just you and me, forever this way!

The Blues

This feeling drapes a serene veil,
Heaviness lingering, thin and pale,
In shadows deep, where silence dwells,
It echoes low, like a midnight bell,
Beneath the weight of a darkened moon,
The heart leads a step astray.

The ache, the struggle & a silent plea,
Empty rooms filled with vacuum,
In muted tones and cloudy dark skies,
Soft as rain, it trickles inside,
With murmurs, the soul can't hide.

The eye sacs have stories to say,
Those tears unseen, unheard, unknown,
Masked expression on that face,
Hands clutch close, but empty stay,
Reaching out as light slips away.

In the hollow, numb heart,
The feeling etches its creative art,

With every tear, the shadows grow,
A storm within, with nowhere to go.
Yet even in this solemn place,
A fragile beauty finds its grace,
With a hidden shade that's ready for a race!

Evolve

A free-spirited wanderer, wild and free,
Lost in dreams, adrift at sea.
You arrived, with a spark unknown,
My *Nishchala Priya,
Steady, patient, strong and intense.

You held my hand when gravity played its
tricks,
You grew into me,
Sewing words that let me pause,
With every song, you brought more cheer,
Every glance refined my feeling,
Rekindling the love I could be, the love in me.

Like a raintree magnificent and high,
You grew into me,

Branching to the open skies,
Holding roots deep inside,
Bending but standing tall,
As mighty winds rush by,
Twining, twisting, wholly bound,
Through all the seasons of the sun.

I wonder,
I believe,
I changed,
I bloomed,
And You grew into me,
Relentless as the river **Sind,
Bending, turning, gushing through
Maneuvering tales untold,
Timeless dance, a quiet prayer,
A lullaby in rushing waves.
Calming the mind,
Reassuring the soul.

Soft as the shades of morning light,
You grew into me,
Fierce as the ocean wild,
Intense as our heart beats,
Loving glance that lets our eyes meet,

Through mist and storm,
Through darkened skies,
Here we stand, woven tight,
Two souls, one life, blossoming love,
I found myself when I found you.

*Nishchala Priya – Steady mind, my love
**Sind – River flowing in Kashmir, source:
Lake Mansarovar

Unknown Feelings

With conviction,
Like a puzzle unveils,
Feels close yet so far,
The gladness that plays like music,
Conversations flow like a river,
A million dimensions open up,
Not knowing can be magical,
Not knowing can be exploratory,
Not knowing can just be not knowing.
There's simplicity,
There's authenticity,
There is joy of company,
Unknown...
Yet so beautiful,
Yet so easy,
So you, so me n so us!

My Favourite Place

Your arms, my favourite place to go,
Time stands still; heartbeats flow.
The lub-dub hums a gentle tune,
A steady rhythm, soft and true,
Shielding my heart in love's warm light,
A magical wrap from day to night.

Nothingness meets a new dimension
Lulling my soul, stirring my mind,
Words fall short and voices fade,
With every touch, a spark is made,
A love so pure, it rises and sways,
In your arms, I find my place,
Wrapped up tight, in warmth & grace.

Through joy and pain,
Through anxiety and cheer,
In every breath, I feel you near,
The darkest nights shine with light,
You are the peace, the calm, the might,
Deep in your eyes, I find my home,
A place where I am never alone.

A gentle retreat, a warm embrace,
A secure hug, my sacred space,
My heart's easiest place to unwind,
So hold me close; don't let me stray behind,
For in your arms, I'm whole, I know
Your arms are my favourite place to go!

Possibilities

In our City
In the bustling streets where dreams collide,
We weave through the chaos, side by side.
In this concrete jungle, our love starts to
grow,
With cell phones clinking on the tables,
We share secret smiles in the morning haze,
Every conversation, every expression,
Becomes the soundtrack to our vibrant tale.

In the soft music in the car and unpredictable
traffic,
Each corner we turn, new adventures await,
A journey together, our own twist of fate,
Through skyscrapers rising, we'll claim our
space,
Hand in hand, we'll still chase the sunset's
hue,
Finding magic in moments, far and near.

So here's to the city, with its endless pace,

Where love blooms in the most unexpected
place,
With every step forward, we'll continue to
grow,
And heartbeat echoes with possibility,
In this urban adventure, just you and me, let's
go.

In the mountain Trail
On winding paths where the wildflowers
sway,
We tread softly through the break of day.
With each step forward on beautiful terrains,
We discover new joys and connections to stay.
The whispering winds hold secrets untold.

Every lake we cross, every mountain we see
Brings us closer together, transcending all
time.
Hand in hand, we traverse steep climbs,
Finding our connection in conversations and
songs,
Each challenge we face on this natural spree,
Strengthens our bond, setting our spirits free.

With the sun setting low, painting skies in
gold,
We pause for a moment, our prayers gently
hold.
As the stars start to twinkle in the twilight's
embrace,
We see endless possibilities in this sacred
place.
In the heart of the wild, we've found our true
home.
For every adventure that lies in the unknown,
In this tapestry of nature, our love has grown.

In Everyday Routines
In the gentle light of morning's embrace,
We rise at the two ends of the city, finding
our place.
Coffee brews softly; the scent fills the air
Tea boils with ginger and lemongrass
In balconies and the rising sun
These simple moments, we're perfectly paired

From morning routines to evening's soft glow,
In the rhythm of life, our affection will flow.

With chores and the mundane, we find joy
anew,
The rush of the day brings its own little
dance,
With shared conversations and laughter,
As we navigate daily life, the world all
around,
In every small gesture, being grateful to each
other.

So here's to the routine, the everyday grind,
Where possibilities flourish and love's
redefined.
In every shared moment, big or small,
Together we thrive; we conquer it all.

Endless Horizons
In the quiet moments, where whispers blend,
Lies a world of possibilities that never end.
Each glance exchanged, a reassurance ignites,
A canvas of dreams beneath starry nights.
With every shared laugh, we break the mould,
Crafting a story that's yet to be told.

With hearts wide open, we'll dare to explore,

The intensity of our love, forever wanting
more.
So here's to the future, with hope in our eyes,
Together we'll soar, like birds in the skies.
For every heartbeat holds promise, you see,
In this beautiful dance, just you and me.

Ecstasy

Beneath the blue blue sky,
The world orates it's story
And every breath blooms,
Like the opening of petals,
Aching in sunlight.

The air is soft with lessons,
As if secrets drift here,
Weightless,
Boundless.
Like a feather left to fly in the universe
Here, within this fragile spell,
I am nothing,
And yet everything.

As night spills across,
I feel the stars come closer,
Their silver sighs settling in my heart,
As if an open-air theatre unravelled,
Drawn into the vastness,
And held subtly but mighty strong.

I drift beyond form,
Beyond name,
Beyond gender,
An overflowing jar of inquisitiveness,
Learning to unlearn, knowing to unknowing.

Acceptance lets boundaries dissolve,
Playing the music of the spheres,
Time loosens, unwinds–
And I am carried on,
Lost in this experience
Of simply Being.

This tranquillity, the universe breathes,
A quiet symphony in each beat,
The soul free flows like rain,
Rising, falling and fading–
A ripple on the endless lake,
Held, then gone, yet forever a part of it all.

The More I Have Of You, The More I Crave

The more I have of you, the more I crave–
Your touch, a whisper of sensations
Lingers like the last note of a song,
Carving quiet rhythms into my soul.

Your presence is a melody I never tire of,
A harmony I carry even in silence.
Every glance feels like the first,
Every word, a thread pulling us closer.

I reach for you, not to hold you still,
But to feel the way you flow through my
world–
An endless tide, gentle yet unyielding.
You are never enough,
Yet, you are everything I need.

My heart stretches wide,
Willing and wanting to reshape for you,
Pondering over the what, when, how
Of loving you better each day.

I watch light play hide and seek on your face,
Be fascinated by the way your voice & eyes
meet
And in your quiet, I listen,
Drawn closer by the gravity of your soul.

I don't want just proximity;
I want to know every atom of you
To feel your depths, to hold your whole.
I want to love you entirely,
To trace every emotion you can be.

The more I have of you,
The more I realise–
You are a limitless universe,
I am happy to orbit forever.
Exploring galaxies unknown,
A traveller in the infinite expanse of our love.

Trust, Love And Friendship

In the depths of heart-to-heart talks where
secrets lay,
Trust weaves its threads in an unknown way.
No promises spoken, no vows to declare,
But a silent bond that often stares.
It's the look in the eye, the steady hand,
A foundation built on love & care
In times of doubt, holding its place,
A strength unseen in a gentle embrace.

Love is the warmth that feeds our souls,
A mystery woven, a story whole.
It grows like ivy, tender and wild,
Soft as a whisper, mild as a child.
It's the hush in the heart, the rhythmic beat,
An uncharted map, where two roads meet.
Through highs and lows, it learns to bend,
A timeless thread that will never end.

Friendship is the laughter that fills the room,
A light in the dark, expelling gloom.

It's the comfort in silence, the joy in sound,
The steady ground when storms surround.
A hand to hold, a voice to guide,
A pillar strong where fears can hide.
It's knowing the worst and staying afloat,
The friend who tells you quote unquote.

Together they rise, braided to a plait,
In the fabric of life, their truths combined.
Trust anchors the heart, love lights the way,
Friendship holds steady through night and
day.
In moments of joy, in trials and pain,
These gifts we keep, even in severe rains,
For life's a journey, fierce and wide,
With trust, love and friendship by our side.

Awakening The Inner Child

There lies a child within my heart
Soft, forgotten and in wonder–
Eyes that once held stars and skies,
Curious mind and full of whys,

Excitement mellowed with passing years,
Lost to logic, cloaked in formats.
Yet in quiet, stolen hours,
I hear laughter, feel the power
A giggle, bright and feather-light,
Cuts through grown-up shades of night,
Whispering tales I left behind,
Of painted seas and hills to climb,

Of dancing storms and wild schemes,
Of freedom, friendship, boundless dreams.

The inner child of mine remains,
Through silent years and passing rains–
She waits for me, in shadows cast,
To take her hand.
She calls me back with gentle hands,
To castles made of ocean sands,
To magic places, green and wild–
Where once I roamed, a free-spirited child.

So hand in hand, we take the leap,
Rediscover joys buried deep–
With open hearts and wide-eyed smiles,
I awaken my inner child!

Inspiration

A song of becoming, an urge to explore,
Waking up to the whisper of morning light,
A spark in the shadows, a flame burning
bright,
It's found in the ember, the leaf as it falls,
The dance of the rain as it answers and calls.
A rhythm, a heartbeat, a wild, endless fire,
Lifting the soul with the breath of inspiration.

Eyes open wider, the world feels anew,
Colours more vivid, each sound ringing true.
In moments once quiet, a symphony grows,
An urge to create where the river now flows.
A pull to belong where the bold spirits
throng.
Boundless and fearless, in dreams we
conspire,
To breathe life into wonder – this gift of
being inspired.

A spark in the stardust, a spark in our soul,
The pull of the universe makes us whole.

A spark that ignites with a glance or a smile,
Turning the simplest of moments worthwhile.
A quiet connection, a language of trust,
As sure as the stars, as gentle as dust.
Bound to the heavens, forever inspired.

It humbles, it strengthens, it peels us to the
core,
As we gather the pieces, rebuild and restore.
The cracks tell a story; the scars bear a name,
All gathered together in a picture on a frame,
In each tear, a lesson, a moment to admire,
A journey to healing, born out of the fire,
Amazed in pain, ready to be inspired.

In paths that we wander, in places we hide,
In the forests, in the valleys,
In the mountains, in the rivers,
In heartbeats, in stardust, in skies vast and
blue.

In hustling cities, amidst traffic and busy
souls,

From the smallest of wonders to dreams we
declare,
The beauty of living – Always &
Everywhere Inspired.

If I Forget
To Tell You Later

If I forget to tell you later,
When the sun dips low and skies grow greyer,
Know this truth that softly stays,
In the silent whispers of my days.

If I forget to tell you later,
When the moonlight fades and shadows cater
To a quiet world where words might sleep,
Know my promises run soul-deep.

If I forget to tell you later,
When the weight of life feels even greater,
Feel my heartbeats; they hum for you,
In rhythms steady, pure and true.

If I forget to tell you later,
And my voice falters, silenced by the hours,
Trust in my actions; they'll always show,
A love that only shines and grows.

If I forget to tell you later,
When time conspires as a sly creator,
Stealing chances to meet your gaze,
Remember, you light my endless days.

If I forget to tell you later,
Through mountains high and valleys
straighter,
Know you're the anchor that keeps me whole,
The steady flame that warms my soul.

If I forget to tell you later,
In fleeting moments or now or later,
No lapse of time, no fleeting day,
Could dim the love I give away.

You are my star, my home, my art,
The constant beat within my heart.
And if all else fades, please always see,
You are the very best part of me.

Invisible Threads

Between two souls, mysteriously sure,
Invisible threads create art & bloom,
Slow and steady or fast and fantastic
Either way, they only grow.

Through early-morning hellos, late-night talks
Weaving dreams of retiring places and more
They linger deep as patterns weave,
Letting the threads beautifully breeze.

Woven in whispers, spun in rhythm,
Invisible threads hold us together,
Pulse in eyes we feel deep inside,
As silent chords play beneath our skin.

A touch, a look, that knows no end–
They knot like bonds, stronger when tight,
From hours passed in quiet ease,
A thousand breaths, a million hearty stares.

From moments shared, from secrets told,

At awesome years of 45 & 43-3/4th,
From laughter's spark and tears we shed,
Precious looms in tandem we spin.

In every silly joke, every deep thought,
In melodies we've both heard,
Misunderstood conversations, little cute
frowns
These close-knit moments will still be our
own.

For in each goodbye, there is a thread,
Of words we spoke, of doubts we happily
shed.
And with each hug, securely, promises we
keep,
Knowing the Invisible threads will take the
leap.

Sweet Obsession

In the beauty of the evening's sunset,
Your presence in my thoughts wraps me with
a glow,
The colours that paint the canvas in gold,
orange and blue
Those Brahminy kites enjoying the thermal of
the evening sky,
Remind me of us, an aura so rare to find.

Walking by the lake and a glimpse, a fleeting
sight,
Forever drawn to who you are,
In your arms is where I dwell.
My shining, beloved Bestest
I'm mesmerised, chasing moments we once
shared,

Your smiles dance in my mind,
Your touch, a gentle, warm caress,
Bound by love's enchanting spell,
Thoughts of you both sweet and deep,
Calms my heart when I'm asleep.

Bound by love's enchanting spell, yet again
You are the thought I can't release,
The restless calm, my steady peace.
You linger close, a breath, a trace–
In every line, I find your face.

A sweet obsession, love's soft spin.
Forever bound, this truth confessed,
My heart's obsession, nonetheless.
In every breath, I'm lost and free–
In loving you, eternally.

Precious Moments

Through tender glances, words unspoken,
Our eyes reveal what hearts have woven,
With lovely smiles that light the air,
We find our world together there.

With the inquisitive stare and cheer,
With boundless joy that draws you near.
A heart that greets with pure embrace,
Love leaves its trail, a gentle trace.

Driving together, your singing on the go,
In melodies, our feelings flow.
The road unfolds, time slows its pace,
As intense love fills our lovely space

In every sip of the classic *LIT we drink,
Our hearts know we are in sync.
The sunset glows, our thoughts blend,
Two souls as one, no place to pretend.

With whispered thoughts, with open fears,
We trust our truths, no masks or tears.
In hugs that linger, hands clutching so deep,
These moments are the ones we keep.

A connection intertwined so tight.
Our love glows like the moon at night.
Once again here we are, just you and me,
In all we are, in all we'll be.

*LIT – Long Island Tea

Restless Pulse

An anxious heart, it beats too fast,
Each thud a question, a shadow cast.
It trembles in the quiet night,
A prisoner of its own delight.

It longs for calm, yet stirs with doubt,
Worried whispers rising out.
Is this the way, the path we're meant,
Or just a fleeting, silent lament?

Every glance, a twist of fate,
A hope that lingers, then turns late.
It aches for certainty, for peace,
For all the worry to finally cease.

But still it beats, though unsure,
In the chaos, it will endure.
For even in its anxious plea,
It knows the strength it holds to be.

And love, though quiet, stands beside,
A steady force, a constant guide.
In every fear, in every start,
Love calms the storm within the heart.

Hope In The Unseen

We walk a path unwritten, hand in hand,
Each step, a quiet promise in our hearts.
No stars to chart our way, no map to follow–
Only the warmth of the stories yet to come.

The future waits like a flower bud,
Each petal holding a mystery, every moment a
choice.
As shadows weave along our path,
And with your heartbeat staying close to
mine

Let the days unfold, just as they will,
With trust in all we do not know.
For love speaks in its own language,
A bond shaped by all that cannot be said.

Here's to the sunrises we have yet to see,
To skies unknown and the songs of open seas.
We walk, unknowing, but gripped by the
pulse of this,
With hope flaring like fire, unbound and
unafraid, together and strong!

The Boundless Journey Of Love

In landscapes uncharted, beneath shifting
skies,
Love moves like wind, untethered, unseen,
Drifting through light and shadow, a quiet
force,
An endless passage traced only by the heart.

It follows no map, respects no edge,
Coursing through laughter and sorrow alike,
Carrying years without counting them,
Finding its way without thought of return.

Every touch a promise, each glance a spark,
Love weaves into memory, into dreams to
come,
Blurring the lines that divide us,
Softening the spaces we keep to ourselves.

It knows no finish, no boundary or end,
Ignoring limits, dissolving lines.
Love is a wanderer, free and wild,
A presence unbound, moving always forward.

So we walk together, through storms and
calm,
Knowing love's journey, infinite, waits ahead.
With every step, our hearts beat as one,
In the silence between, our souls are led.

Being With You

Being with you is a quiet kind of magic,
A calm in the storm, hope in a world so
chaotic.
Your touch is the map my heart follows home,
With you, I am never alone.

Your laughter, a melody soft yet strong,
A rhythm that pulls me, where I belong.
The world feels lighter, skies more blue,
When I lose myself in being with you.

Your smile is a haven, a shelter, a spark,
Walking me gently through life's shadowed
arc.

With every embrace, I feel time slow,
A love so steady, it endlessly grows.

No mountain too high, no valley too deep,
Together, our promises we'll always keep.
Being with you, my soul's sweetest song,
A melody where I truly belong.
Being with you is the story I write,
Each chapter glows with endless light.
No other tale could feel so true
For every moment now, begins with you.

Moonlit Whispers

Of beauty
Of tranquillity
Of love
Of trust
Of possibilities
Of oneness

The twinkle in the eyes
The wonder
The sensations
Enchanted – spellbound
Tip-toed, ready for a dance
Arms encapsulated
Connected hearts
Love to love
Vulnerability in honesty

Connecting the souls
In the moment
Pure, subtle, uninterrupted

A silhouette ...rarely seen
And I believe it's you
And I know it's you
And I realise it's you
And in this moment, it's only you!

Moments And Memories

Moments flicker like stars in the night,
Brief and fleeting, yet shining in delight.
A laughter shared, a tear held close,
The quiet joys we cherish most.

Memories grow like vines on a wall,
Climbing through seasons, we hold them all.
The scent of rain, the warmth of a hand,
A melody played by time's quiet band.

A sunrise kissed with hues of gold,
A story shared, a secret told.
In the folds of time, these treasures stay,
Whispering softly of yesterday.

A walk by the lake, the world fades away,
Your smile outshines the golden day.
A shared secret, a fleeting kiss,
Little moments that feel like bliss.

A quiet laugh, a stolen glance,
A twirl beneath the moon's soft dance.
The way your hand finds mine with ease,
The hush of whispers in the breeze.

Through every path, both bright and steep,
Moments awake from where they sleep.
Like echoes dancing in the breeze,
They shape our lives with gentle ease.

These tiny threads, they gently bind,
Precious moments etched in time.
A beautiful story written in simple ways,
In little memories, we find our days.

You Flow Like A Poem

You flow like a poem, soft and serene,
A whisper of beauty, a luminous dream.
Each word, a ripple, in rivers of time,
Your presence, a cadence, a rhythm divine.

Your smile, the stanza where joy takes its
flight,
A melody dancing in warm, golden light.
Your touch, like a verse, both tender and
strong,
A balm to my soul, a comforting song.

Your eyes hold the sonnets the stars long to
sing,
With depths of the ocean and grace of the
spring.

You wander through moments, both fleeting
and true,
Weaving a tapestry richer than hue.

You flow like a poem, and I am the page,
Where your love leaves its mark, from youth
through to age.
In your presence, I flourish; my heart takes its
form,
In the warmth of your words, I am endlessly
born.

I Belong To You

Like rivers dancing their way to the sea,
A bond unbroken, wild yet free.
Through every sunrise, every starry view,
My heart whispers softly, I belong to you.

In your gaze, I find my place,
A tender warmth, a timeless space.
No need for words; your warmth speaks true,
In every breath, I belong to you.

Like mountains standing, bold and tall,
You're my strength when I fear to fall.
Your love, a path both bright and new,
Guiding me home – I belong to you.

Through endless skies and seasons' turns,
For your embrace, my soul will yearn.
Forever, my heart beats its vow to renew,
With every pulse – I belong to you.

This vastness of the universe, in time, in space
In every touch, in every trace
Through all that is fleeting & all that is true,
A feeling that's certain – I belong to you.

You

Beneath the stars, a tale unfolds
Heart set high where the rivers flow.
Among the cliffs, a story takes flight,
Vast and eternal as the alpine height.
Amid rugged trails, your spirit feels free,
Nature, she adores you, in all glee.
In your being, the summits sing,
Soft winds carry the charisma you bring.
Happiness blooms in your presence,
A melody of love in perfect balance.
Nestled in the heights, endless dreams reside,
Kissed by the clouds and wildflowers beside.
A bond with nature, untamed and true,
Rising like the peaks, truly the awesome –
You.

Where We'll Wander

She speaks of mountain trails so steep,
Where clouds and cliffs in silence sleep.
'With every step, I'll be your guide,
Together we'll conquer the mountainside'.

She dreams of shores where the waves play
free,
Barefoot laughter by the rolling sea.
'We'll chase the tide till the sun is low,
And dance in the rhythm where the breezes
go'.

She whispers of forests, calm and green,
Where sunlight weaves through a golden
sheen.
'We'll wander the woods, just you and me,
Listening to nature's symphony'.

She smiles at thoughts of meals we'd make,
Spices blending, scents awake.
'In your arms, as the flavours blend,
Our laughter will turn kitchens to heaven'.

She speaks of a couch, a cosy retreat,
Where the world feels distant, our hearts
complete.
'Curled up together, let time stand still,
In your embrace, the world is fulfilled'.

She laughs at the thought of a marathon's
start,
'Our feet in sync, one racing heart.
Through every mile, through every stride,
Your strength, my joy – our worlds collide'.

She twirls to the rhythm of songs unsung,
Her voice, a melody, forever young.
'Let's dance till the stars fall from the sky,
Sing our love till the echoes fly'.

She sees her dreams in shades of you,
Every moment, a bond renewed.
Through every life experience, through all we
do,
Her only wish: 'To be with you'.

Effortless Joy

With you, the world feels lighter still,
No need for pretence, no climb, no hill.
Each moment flows, like a gentle stream,
A life of ease, like a cherished dream.

Laughter springs from the simplest glance,
Every step together, a carefree dance.
Time melts away in your steady embrace,
Happiness blooms; it finds its place.

No need for words, yet they spill so free,
A language of love, just you and me.
Through sunlit days or skies of grey,
With you, my heart will always stay.

Time slows its march when you are near,
Moments stretch, yet crystal clear.
A touch, a glance, the simplest things,
Turn mundane days into radiant springs.

So here I am, where peace is true,
Where life feels bright – because of you.

Together Now And Forever

Beneath the same sun, we stand apart,
Two distant shores, but one beating heart.
Our dreams merge, though paths divide,
A love too vast for space to hide.

Your voice still echoes in quiet air,
A whispered promise, a tender care.
Though hands can't touch, our souls still
meet,
In every thought, in every beat.

The world may keep our bodies away,
Yet in my mind, you always stay.
A love like ours defies the tide,
Together forever, though worlds collide.

We carve our vows in the stars above,
A testament to boundless love.
No force can dim what's meant to shine,
You'll always be eternally mine.

When lifetimes fade and time is through,
I'll find my way back home to you.
In every realm, in every place,
Forever bound by love's embrace.

For though we live where fate has drawn,
Our hearts are homes we'll lean upon.
No walls, no miles can ever sever,
For we are together, now and forever.

The Pause

Not an end, but a quiet delay,
A fleeting shadow in love's bright day.
Your hand slips, yet it doesn't let go,
A whispering promise the heart will know.

The miles may stretch, the skies may part,
But distance can't sever what binds the heart.
Our laughter echoes, our dreams remain,
Threads of gold in love's refrain.

The clock ticks slowly, yet time will weave,
A path back home, though hearts may grieve.
For even the moon must bid the sun
A gentle farewell when the day is done.

This pause, this stillness, is but a test,
A moment to cherish what we possess.
For when we reunite, the world will see,
How love endures, unbroken, free.

Comfortably Numb

The buzz of the city around us,
A restless, pulsing beat,
Lights flicker in the distance
As we stare at the busy streets

Drifting in a sea of quiet,
Where nothing cuts too deep,
The world hums softly, distant,
Like a lullaby for sleep.

Hand so warm beside me,
But there's a faded spark–
A quiet we didn't speak of earlier,
A dimming in the dark.

We move through neon rivers,
Past strangers lost in flow,
The world, a rushing current–
But we're drifting, moving slow.

You say something beside me,
A question lost in haze,
But I just nod in answer,
Eyes glazed in distant gaze.

The chaos forms a cradle,
A shield around this calm—
Comfortably numb, I linger
In your quiet, cooling palm.

And though the city roars on,
And hearts beat loud and clear,
We walk along together,
Alone but always near.

Steel towers rise above me,
Their lights a dulling glow,
A thousand windows watching,
But none of them will know.

No highs, no lows, just drifting
In quiet, muted calm—
Comfortably numb, we wander
Through the city's steady hymn

No ache, no want, no need, no sorrow,
Just peace where once was pain–
Comfortably numb, I linger,
In calm, of an unbroken rainbow.

Journey Of Connected Souls

Across endless landscapes, they wander,
Not bound by borders, by clocks or miles,
Drawn together by something deep, unseen—
A silent calling, like rivers pulled to the sea.

In lifetimes past, they have met in fleeting
glances,
In familiar laughter, in moments of stillness,
And though the forms may shift and fade,
Their hearts know the language beyond
words.

Together in all realms, both near and far,
In dreams, in whispers, in the pulse of stars—
They meet in worlds woven and unspoken,
Tethered across the spaces between.

They journey onward, apart and together,
Through joy, through sorrow, weaving threads
anew,
Ever connected, a flame that won't be
dimmed,
Two souls bound to meet, again and again.

From Sunrise To Sunset

Together we tread where the earth kisses the
sky,
From sunrise to sunset, as hours quietly fly.
Snowflakes whisper, forests sigh in the breeze,
Through seasons we wander, in moments of
ease

Snow-peaked mountains, their majesty
untamed,
Stand as our witness, their beauty unnamed.
Golden skies stretch as the day greets its
close,
While wildflowers bloom where the cold river
flows.

By campfires we gather, their warmth a soft
glow,
Singing with the wind, as shadows grow.
A meteor shower streaks across the night,
Stars paint the heavens in shimmering light.

Together we marvel at nature's grand art,
Its beauty etched in the map of our hearts.
Each trail we walk, each story we weave,
A tapestry of moments we never will leave.

Each step, a bond, a strength that we share,
Lifting, holding, with hearts laid bare.
Doing nothing, yet so much we create,
Moments eternal, where souls resonate.

And as the sun dips, with stars shining near,
We hold to the hope of each coming year.
This time, these days, together we'll stay,
From sunrise to sunset, come what may!

Gratitude In Verse

To you, my love, this heart takes flight,
A burning star in endless night.
For every moment, every care,
For simply being always there.

You shaped my soul with patient hands,
Ground me to where I stand.
Through days and months, you helped me
grow,
A deeper strength than I could know.

Together we've carved memories bright,
In shared horizons, day and night.
From laughter's peaks to silence deep,
You're the keeper of the dreams I keep.

Your voice, a hymn that soothes my pain,
Your gaze, the sun that breaks my rain.
Each whispered story, each daring stride,
Built the universe where I reside.

For now, I treasure every hour,
Each fleeting second, each fragile flower
Of time we're given – blessed and rare,
A sacred bond beyond compare.

No matter where our journeys end,
Thank you, love, for all that you blend.
For every blessing, every start,
My reason, my all – treasured, in my heart!